Being
Black

Donald R. Guillory

ISBN: 099762812X
ISBN-13: 978-0-9976281-2-8
Cover design by Donald R. Guillory

Twitter: @donguillory

DEDICATION

This work is dedicated to my parents, Donald and Glenda for giving me the strength to always be myself, to my wife, Claudia, for her constant encouragement, to my daughter, Arya, whom I hope many of the issues and hardships faced by previous generations will not be revisited upon her, to all of my friends who kept me motivated, and to all of the "Tokens" who carry the banner of their identity as a sword and a shield to battle the ignorance of the world.

My friend James, or as he is more affectionately known; "White James," once asked me "What's it like to be black?" I turned to him and replied, "Well, imagine you are invited to a party and while there you are constantly being watched. You don't really know many of the people in attendance so you look around to get a sense of the room. You see people getting drinks and food. You walk over and grab something to eat only to be told you can't have anything. When you ask why, you are accused of being aggressive or confrontational. People start talking. Discouraged, you walk away and stand in a corner only to be told by another attendee of the party that you cannot occupy that space. You try to strike up a conversation with someone, anyone who is willing to talk with you only to be met with blank stares and confused looks as though you are speaking a different language. You look for an exit so you can go home, but are stopped as your hand touches the doorknob and asked "why are you leaving?"

"What do you mean?" James asked looking for clarification.

"Well, it's complicated."

It's complicated to define, complicated to understand, and a complicated existence to experience.

It's about trying to learn who you are with little to no resources.

It's being told there are equal opportunities, yet having obstacles thrown on your path and facing a heavy headwind.

It's receiving "The Talk."

It's not being allowed to wear a hoodie without being suspicious.

It's hearing the word "Ghetto" said by your peers and knowing that they are not discussing urban renewal.

It's "fitting the profile" when you don't even come close to matching the description.

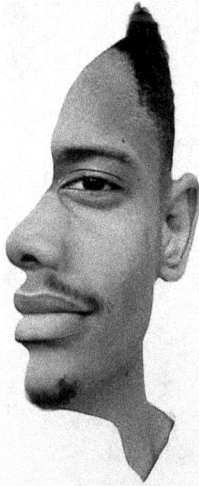

It's about not being given the benefit of the doubt and hardly ever presumed innocent.

It's about being asked "is your father in the home" and not "what does your father do for a living?"

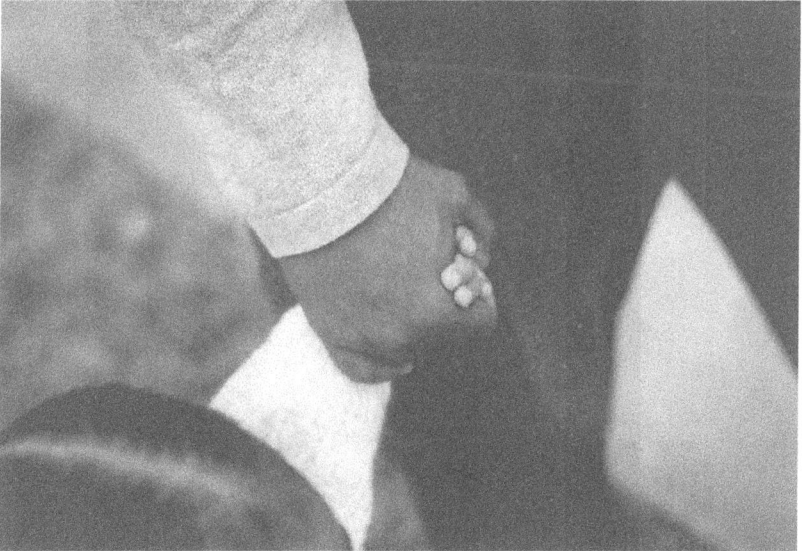

It's having your high school English teacher tell you that
Families like that on the "Cosby Show" are complete fantasy.

It's about having coworkers whisper "affirmative action hire" or being told that the only reason you got into college is because of your skin color… never mind what your transcripts might state or your experience may be.

It's about arriving at your new job and having a coworker sprinkle into conversation several times about how he voted for Obama.

It's a stranger at a football game asking your thoughts on Colin Kaepernick as the anthem singer is grabbing the microphone.

It's having your white classmates turn around and look at you when the teacher asks your social studies class about Africa.

It's attending schools in the South where your black history lessons are limited to MLK and slavery.

It's never reading a black author in your English Courses until your first semester of college.

It's being assembled in a room of your peers to watch the OJ verdict and when the words "Not Guilty" come out of the foreman's lips, the principal's son turns to you and states "That's alright, the Klan will get payback for this."

It's walking into a barbershop and before the bell over the door hits its second jingle, the barber shouts out "I don't cut your hair."

It's tracing your family history on the continent to well before the American republic was an idea but being treated as a second-class citizen.

It's whenever you complain about an injustice in America and a bigot responds with "Go back to Africa!"

It's having someone feel comfortable enough with your in-laws to ask them why they allowed their child to marry "a black."

It's being afraid to call the police when someone is breaking into your home at 3 in the morning.

It's seeing a black kid alone and praying that they make it home safely.

It's growing up around people proudly wearing or flying the symbols of their "heritage" and seeing people proudly post on social media about their "Plantation Weddings."

It's not being able to enjoy a horror movie growing up because you know that anyone who looks like you will not make it past the first act.

It's worrying about some random person coming across your FB Live or Youtube feed and feeling compelled to type the word "Nigger" in the comment section.

It's being on a college campus and regularly asked more about what sport you play than what you are majoring in.

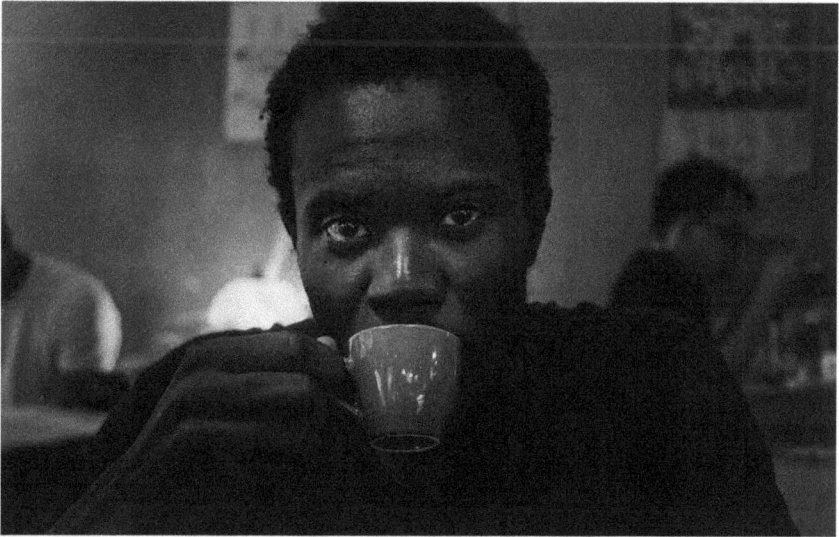

Cringing when you hear the word "articulate."

Having a well-meaning academic advisor tell you that you should take African American history because "it would be perfect for you."

It's listening to Hip-Hop with your non-black friends and waiting to see if they will actually recite all of the lyrics.

It's having a student bring you a straw hat they found during PE and joke that "you can use this when you return to the fields."

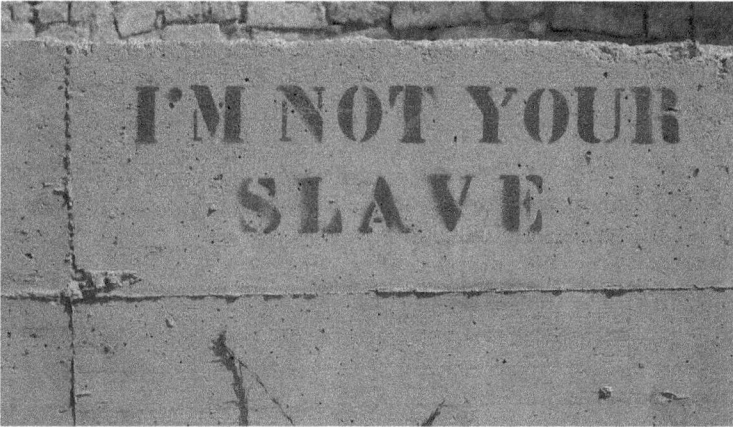

It's watching a black athlete be referred to as cocky or arrogant when his white peers are deemed "confident."

It's moving into a predominantly white neighborhood and having the residents ask how you can afford to live there.

It's not being surprised at a not guilty verdict in cases of police brutality.

It's hearing "What would Dr King say" whenever there is a moment of social strife.

It's not being able to protest in any "acceptable" way other than sitting down and shutting up... hold on... that one has just been crossed off the list...

It's rolling your eyes and letting out a deep sigh when hearing the term "post-racial."

It's the frustration of witnessing as someone's "oppression cosplay" / neoblackface is taken and accepted as a valid experience of what it means to be black.

It's when every fiber of your being wants to throw that punch but doing so will make you a statistic or support someone's myopic and bigoted claims that you are "violent."

It's hoping to one day reenact the doorbell scene from *There's something about Mary* or *Bad Boys 2* when my daughter is picked up for a date.

It's white NCOs not wanting to salute you and black NCOs
flocking to you in order to show respect.

It's having to hear "What about White History Month?" each and every February…

It's not batting an eye when Kanye went off script during the Hurricane Katrina telethon.

It's not getting equal treatment with a doctor because of the stereotype that black people have higher tolerances for physical pain.

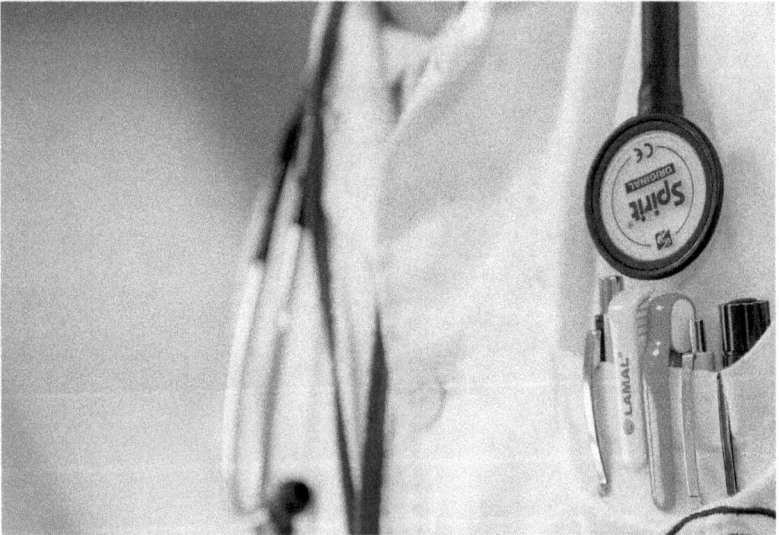

It's not seeking mental health care or counseling because "that ain't for us."

It's not being able to laugh too loudly in public or on a train.

It's having to balance being an ambassador and a mascot.

It's embracing a stigma as a method of survival.

It's looking at a map and crossing off places that you can't travel safely or visit without being harassed based solely on their history with people of color.

It's knowing that the same people who cheer you while dribbling, catching, or throwing a ball will quickly abandon you once you take up a cause that makes them uncomfortable.

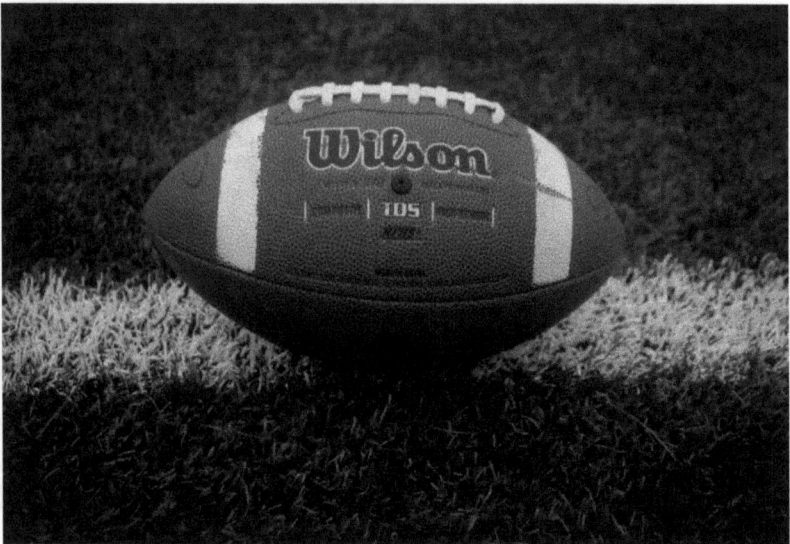

It's noticing how a woman holds her purse tighter when you get onto the elevator.

It's having any number of black students refer to you as "uncle" or "auntie" because you happen to be the only teacher at their school.

It's knowing that Charlottesville was not an isolated incident or an anomaly.

It's being the first suspect when something is missing in the dorm.

It's security refusing you entry into a frat party despite showing your invitation and frat brothers vouching for you. As you walk by, the security guard states "I'm not going to be held responsible for anything that happens."

It's being told "You're acting white" because of your speech, choice of dress, musical taste, or hell… anything that doesn't fit someone's idea of what you should be.

It's being met with odd looks when you enter a room that signify "unwelcome."

It's hearing peers at nearby tables during SAT prep remark "I don't know why he's even here… they get to go to college for free anyway…"

Carrying the weight of previous generations' struggles and knowing that you can't risk screwing up what they fought so hard for.

It's your boss praising you for your hard work and recognizing your contributions to the company before walking you into the breakroom to show you tables with several watermelons displayed, before remarking that he knows how much your people love them.

It means not being able to express an emotion other than anger or apathy, otherwise you are considered "weak."

It's having a bomb threat called in on your University because you are the first black person to attend.

It's that joy and raucous cheering coming from the stands when you accept your diploma despite the PA informing the crowd to wait until the end to cheer.

It's being put on trial for your own murder

It's being told over the phone that there are plenty of vacancies only to be told that there has either been a mistake or the last apartment was just rented when you show up in person.

V CANCY

It means you're not shocked by any of the issues brought up in these pages because they are the same ones you have faced or know someone has faced.

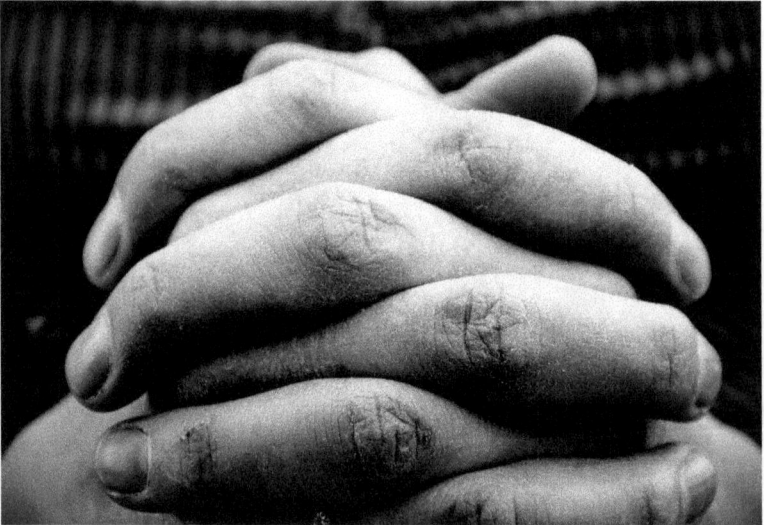

It's being pulled over by the police and not knowing if you will make it home and your white friend joking about how the only way you were able to be let off during the police stop is because he was in the car.

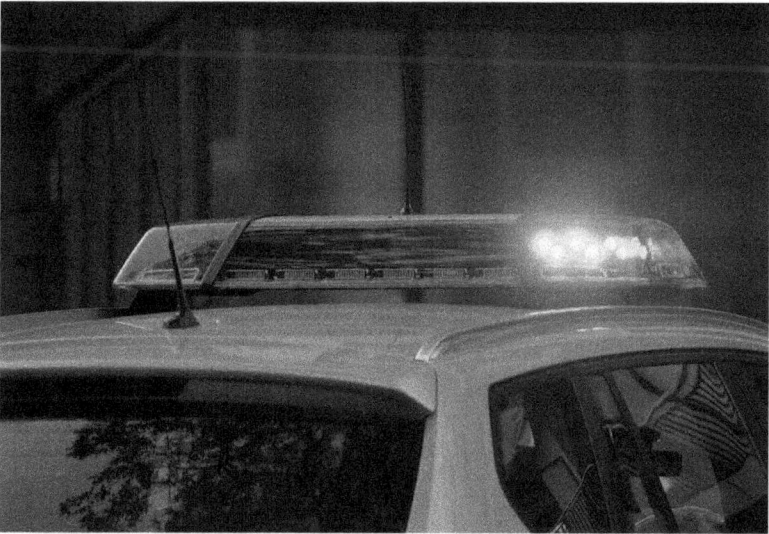

It means being given a nickname because yours is "hard to pronounce" before listening to selections of Tchaikovsky or Rachmaninoff in your music class.

It's being at a basketball or football game on campus and repeatedly asked each game as to which sport you played when you attended the school… "You're pretty big… are you sure you didn't play something here… You wrestled, right…"

It's being set up on a blind date by friends with the only other black person that they know of because "you two will get along so well together…"

It's how Grand Master Flash's "Message" still resonates with you… "Sometimes I wonder how I keep from going under."

It's

knowing

that   this

list   will

never

be

complete

It's understanding why the caged bird sings even without reading any lines of Maya Angelou.

It's feeling the pain in that one black tear that Denzel sheds on screen.

It's understanding the tears flowing from your own eyes as you watch the election night results of November 4th, 2008.

It's the realization and psychological trauma of knowing it could have been you in any one of those videos or your name as the newest hashtag.

#yournamehere

It's explaining for the umpteenth time that "Black Lives Matter" means too… not more…

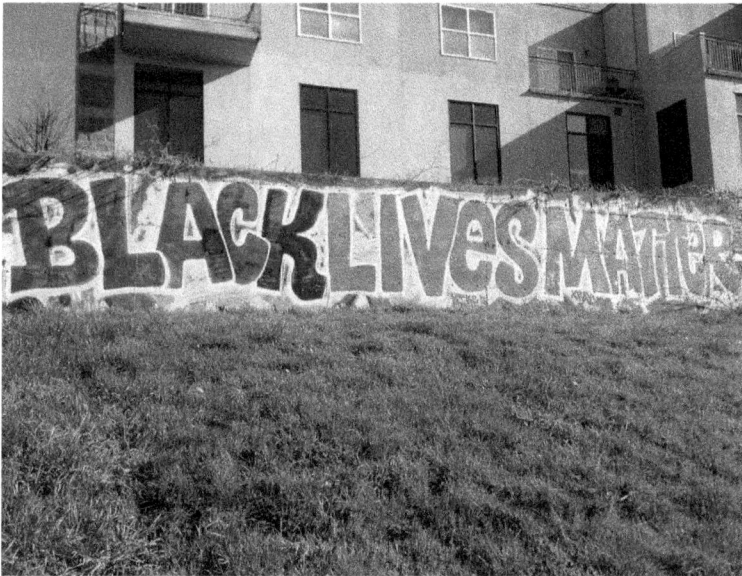

It's hearing "Don't worry, we only shoot black people" and having someone excuse it as a joke or sarcasm. Your safety is ridiculed and seen as a punchline.

It's being met with disbelief when you tell someone that you speak more than English.

It's having the right answers only to discover that the
questions have been changed.

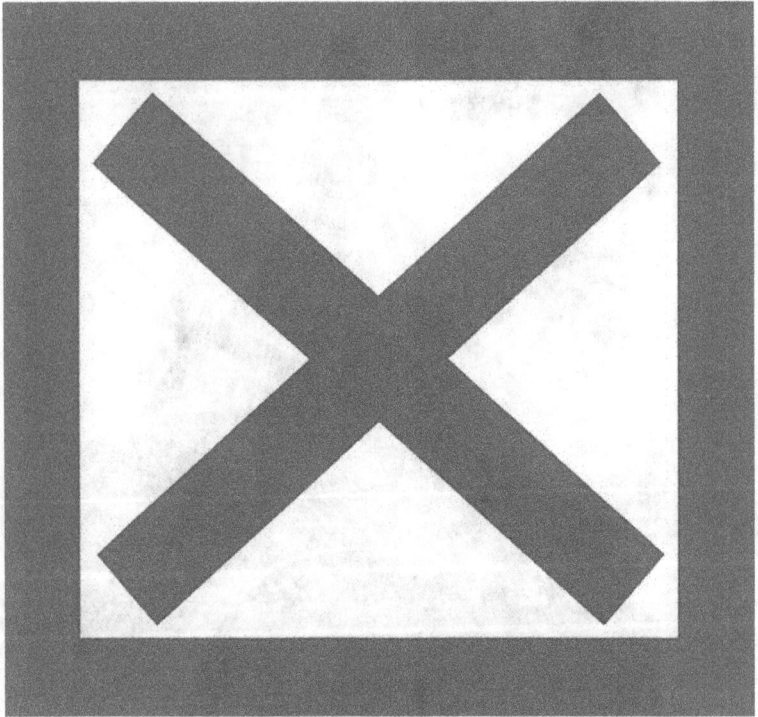

It's an Italian family fighting to take a photo with you because you are the first black person from America that they have ever met.

It's exhausting…

It's knowing that you will instinctively turn up the volume whenever you hear the words "Cash Money taking over the 99 and the 2000."

It's having diapers in the backseat of your car (when you don't have kids) just in case you get pulled over by the police.

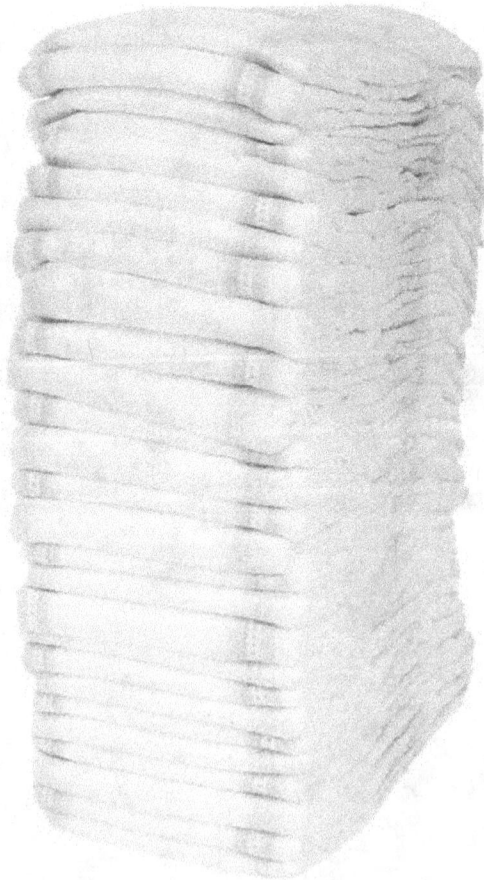

It's having a grandfather who was visited by the Klan on more than one occasion because he was housing members of SNCC and "riling up the local negroes with talk of voting."

It's rebuilding your family church after is has been burned down for organizing voter registration drives and "agitation" only to have it burned down again.

It's passing up a better life in NY because of the guilt you have in your family not being able to escape Jim Crow.

Guillory

It means not being able to wear your uniform in public due to how the locals might feel about a negro officer.

It means fighting for a country that isn't always willing to fight for you.

It is not being able to travel freely.

It's not being able to assemble into a group larger than 3-4 people without arising suspicion.

It's knowing that the question "Where you from?" isn't always an innocent question.

It's recognizing the difference between one hand on the hip versus two.

WARNING

It's knowing that "being invited to the cookout" doesn't involve food.

It's knowing that if you don't know how to play spades that you don't sit down at the table.

It's knowing that you don't just eat anyone's potato salad and for that matter, you don't eat anything at the company potluck.

It's triumph and sorrow… it's laughing to keep yourself from crying, it's certainty and confusion… In the words of James Baldwin, "To be a negro in this country and to be relatively conscious is to be in a rage almost all of the time…" "What's it like to be black?" you ask… well… It's complicated…

ABOUT THE AUTHOR

Don Guillory is an historian, US Army Veteran, educator, and author of "The Token Black Guide: Navigations Through Race in America." He is a graduate of Georgia Southern University, where he earned his Master of Arts in History, and Arizona State University where he earned his Master of Education. He currently teaches courses on history, race, and culture in Arizona where he lives with his wife and daughter.

Twitter: @donguillory

www.ingramcontent.com/pod-product-compliance
Lightning Source LLC
Chambersburg PA
CBHW050543280326
41933CB00011B/1695